REFLECTIONS

ON THE JESUS PRAYER

by A Priest of the Byzantine Church

Dimension Books
Denville, New Jersey

Published by Dimension Books, Inc.
Denville, New Jersey 07834

Dedication

To my Father and my Mother; and to all my brothers and sisters "behind the blue door."

All-Holy Mother of God, save us.

ISBN 0-87193-070-6
Copyright ©1978 by Dimension Books Inc.

TABLE OF CONTENTS

Page

Author's Foreword

These *Reflections* do not pretend to be a complete setting forth of hesychast spirituality, nor are they the words of a *staretz*. They are nothing more than what the title literally suggests: reflections of someone who for six years now has been doing his best to follow the hesychast way of life. To the best of my knowledge, they are in conformity with Holy Tradition and the teachings of the fathers. If in any way they deviate therefrom, it is through lack of knowledge, not through lack of docility, I hope.

It is difficult for an anonymous author to thank publicly the people who have helped him, without jeopardizing his anonymity. Those who read this book knowing who wrote it will, I trust, understand. All of you who are that close to me have helped me, in some way, and I thank you all. Special thanks are due to the editor of the periodical in which these *Reflections* originally appeared and to the men who encouraged me to publish.

I pray for all who may read this. Please remember me, also.

1. "God is With Us"

If you were to conduct a survey of Orthodox Christians, asking them what they thought was the special message or emphasis of their tradition, as distinguished from other Christian traditions, you would probably get a variety of answers. But I think they would tend to boil down into one key concept. I think that concept is well expressed in a phrase from our worship: "God is with us."[1] Or, in another liturgical phrase, "God is the Lord, and has revealed Himself to us."[2] I would say, without any hesitation, that this is the most characteristic feature of Eastern Christian piety and spirituality: an awareness of the *presence of God*. Man lives and works and has his being in a kind of Temple: we are always in the presence of a Mystery, a Sacrament; we are always on the borderline between time and

---

1. From Great Compline.
2. From daily Matins.

9

eternity, between matter and spirit, between the visible and the invisible. This is a way of saying that Eastern Christian piety is basically *mystical,* for a mystic is a person who has a more or less vivid sense of the Presence of God.

There are many ways in which God manifests Himself to us. But they can be summed up under three headings: creation, revelation, and self. Creation and revelation are God coming at us from outside; *self* is God coming at us from inside. And I want to consider each of these in turn.

1. First, *creation.* When I said that man lives in a sort of Temple, this is what I had mostly in mind. The physical space in which we live: our human environment, especially our fellow human beings; the houses and cities and societies and cultures we build and create for ourselves; the land we work on to bring forth food; the earth with its many minerals, the hundreds of thousands of species of trees and plants it produces, the equally numerous varieties of animal life it sustains; the sea in its vastness and power; the air and the sky, and the mighty

phenomena of clouds and winds and thunder and lightning and storms; and the huge vastness of space: sun, moon, planets, stars, galaxies—all this which the ancient Greeks (and our modern scientists) call the *cosmos*. And this is our Temple. Or, to use another word which the Greek Fathers like, it is an *icon*, a picture. The man who looks upon this vast and beautiful creation sees a representation of God. But a good icon does more than merely represent: it in some way makes present the person who is depicted. And so the cosmos actually makes God present to us: it is transparent, so to speak, and God shines through. The cosmos is luminous with the Presence of God. Or, to express it in yet another way, the cosmos is a *sacrament*, a visible, external sign (i.e., outside of and beyond ourselves) that God has made and given to us, by which He makes Himself powerfully present to us. And the person who sees Creation in this way, and who uses it and makes it his own, is indeed drinking deeply of Divine Grace. The Feast of Epiphany with its solemn blessing of the waters, which ends with a sprinkling of the four points of the compass, that is to say, the four corners of the universe, and then with the ensuing blessing of people and houses and animals and belongings, and with the actual drinking of the blessed water—this is the Eastern Church's liturgical expression of this cosmic mysticism, this drinking deep of God through His Creation.

2. But Creation itself is not enough of a manifestation of God. It is so easy to mistake the icon of God for God Himself. And paganism, both ancient and modern, inevitably falls into this tragic mistake. Man needs to know that God is beyond and above His Creation, that He is not just a cosmic force, but a person who wills and loves and acts mightily.

And so God has manifested Himself to us in a second way: through Revelation. He has intervened personally in history, and has spoken clearly to man, telling us who and what He is: to Adam, to Noah, to Abraham, to Moses, to the Prophets. He has revealed Himself not only in word but in act: bringing Abraham out of Mesopotamia into Canaan, bringing Israel out of Egypt into the Promised Land by a series of astounding miracles, rewarding and punishing Israel all through its varied and dramatic history, and finally sending us His own Son, in the fullness of time, to speak to us, to suffer and die for us, to rise on the Third Day, to ascend into heaven, to pour forth His Holy Spirit upon the Apostles, and to establish His Holy Church.

Thus, by a series of mighty acts, God has revealed Himself to men throughout history, has taught us His Truth, has guided us in the right way, and has made Himself permanently present to us in His Church, through His Holy Spirit. The Church is, you might say, the vehicle of His revelation. He continues to reveal Himself through the Church: in Holy Tradition, that collective memory of the Church which keeps alive the great events and truths which Christ revealed to us; we keep handing them down from generation to generation, meditating on them, re-thinking and re-explaining them, always gaining new insights into them and developing them, and communicating them to one another. It is thus that we, the Church, are the vehicle of God's Revelation.

A special place in Holy Tradition is occupied by the Scriptures. Every day in the Psalms, the Epistles and the Gospels, our Liturgy sets forth God's inspired word before us. When we hear Scripture, either when we read it ourselves privately, or when we hear it read to us in groups that gather to pray, and most especially when we hear it read in that public and sacramental gathering of the Church that we call the Liturgy, we are present at a revelation of God. And most especially when the Holy Gospels are read, we are listening to our Savior's own words to us. When the priest or deacon in Church opens the Gospels and proclaims them, Christ is standing in our midst, uttering once again His powerful and life-giving Word. And if we listen with the ears of faith, we are filled and healed by Him, just as He healed the sick in Galilee.

But God reveals Himself to us through His Church in an even more powerful way. And that is in His sacraments and in His worship, and most especially in the Divine Liturgy, which is both

14

sacrament and worship. Here the risen, living Christ is again truly present in His own Body, in the mystery of the Bread and the Wine. He who touches these Holy Things touches God. He who eats and drinks of these Holy Things is fed and nourished by God. We become flesh of His flesh, bone of His bone. This is revelation indeed! "He who eats my flesh and drinks my blood *abides in Me, and I in him.*" The borderline between time and eternity, between matter and spirit, between the visible and the invisible, here breaks down. In the Eucharist, it is all one: man and God come together completely and perfectly in the same Body: the Body of Christ, the body of each one who communicates of Him. "Blessed is He Who comes in the name of the Lord; the Lord is God, and has *revealed Himself* to us," we sing when the Holy Things are brought forth at Communion time in the Divine Liturgy.

And such is Revelation.

3. But these manifestations of God's Presence, whether in Creation or in Revelation, however powerful and beautiful they may be, can only be ef-

fective if I, the beholder and receiver of God's grace, can indeed behold and receive. I must have eyes that can see and ears that can hear, and a mind to understand. I must be opened up from within. God must manifest Himself to me not only from *outside* myself, but also from *inside* myself. And here we come to the third way in which God comes at us. For we can recognize Him in His external manifestations only if we possess Him within ourselves, or rather, if we are possessed by Him. For it is only if the Holy Spirit dwells in us that we have the eyes and the ears to see and hear God outside of us. We must be God-like before we can recognize God.

This third mode of Divine manifestation is, as you can see, extremely important. On it hinges the whole effectiveness of God's grace. Only to Spirit-filled people does the cosmos manifest God. Without Spirit-filled people there could have been no revelation, no Israel, no Prophets, no Christ, for Christ could have been born only of a Spirit-filled Mother, and He Himself is full of the Holy Spirit. Without Spirit-filled people there could be no Church, no

Tradition, no sacraments. "The kingdom of God is within you." It has to come from *inside*. Otherwise it's no good: it's just a dead collection of dogmas and philosophical speculations, rites and formalities. But "the Spirit gives life." It is God present *within* me that makes everything else real for me. He creates and reveals from *within*.

For God is indeed present within the Self. If He is present within the cosmos, then certainly He is present within this miniature cosmos which is the Self. If the cosmos is a Temple, an icon of God, then certainly the human person is also. St. Paul tells us that we are Temples of the Holy Spirit. The Book of Genesis says that God breathed His Spirit into Man when He created him, and, further, that He made him in His own image (i.e., His icon). There can be no doubt that man is Temple and Icon of God. This is the great mystery of Self, and the basis of that love of Self which the Commandment of the New Covenant bids us to have: to love my Self, and to love all other Selves as my Self. The Self is the Icon and the Temple of the living God.

The Self is a miniature cosmos. But there is an important difference between man, the "little cosmos," and the greater cosmos. Man is *free*. He can accept or reject God's presence within himself. He can consent to be possessed by the Holy Spirit, or He can drive Him out, desecrating the Temple which is him-Self, desecrating other Selves.

And this freedom, despite the negative possibilities that it entails, constitutes our great glory. For God is present in galaxies and clouds and cabbages without any conscious acceptance on their part. But if God is present in man, it is because man has *desired* and *accepted* this Presence. And this is a great and glorious thing.

And in the moment that man says to God, "Come. I want You. Send Your Spirit into me"—in that moment the whole of Creation and of Revelation becomes alive. It is in that moment that God comes and fills the whole Temple with His shining, glorious Presence. It is then that "God is with us." What a tremendous mystery: God waits upon man's free consent in order to manifest Himself! God waits for the creature's invitation in order to make Himself present.

18

2. The Prayer of The Heart

God is present *within* us; He manifests Himself in *our* Self, and this inner manifestation of God is all-important; there is no religious life, no life of the Spirit without this; our sanctification and our salvation hinge on this. Moreover, this manifestation of God in us depends on ourselves: it takes place only if we want it to take place.

And this leads us now more properly into our subject matter. If the Eastern Church emphasizes the presence of God-with-us, it particularly emphasizes His presence in this third way, i.e., in the Self. We have said that Eastern Christian spirituality is *mystical.* We can here add that it is *contemplative.* And the contemplative spirituality of the Christian East revolves almost exclusively around one doctrine of the Orthodox Catholic Church: the indwelling of the Holy Trinity. And, further, this spirituality, as it has developed in more recent centuries, has

21

centered (again almost exclusively) on a specific *method* and *tradition* of prayer: the Prayer of the Heart, or the Jesus Prayer, or *hesychasm*. All three terms refer to the same thing, but highlight different aspects of it: "Prayer of the Heart" emphasizes the *method*; "Jesus Prayer" puts the stress on the *words* of the Prayer; "hesychasm" is a convenient word to use for the school of spirituality that has arisen from this Prayer.

I want to emphasize at the outset that the Jesus Prayer is not just some faddish little practice limited to a few chosen souls in cloistered monasteries, who have fastened on some one point of Christian tradition to the exclusion of everything else. It is not merely a *practice*. It is an *approach* to the whole Christian life, and it is possible for everybody. And, precisely because it is such a complete approach to the Christian life, *it can be substituted by any other good spirituality*. The hesychast who claims that *his* way is the only way is not a good Christian, nor even a good hesychast. Hesychasm has always modestly asserted that it is a *good* way to pray, but that there are other good ways.

That having been said, let us talk about the Prayer of the Heart itself. First, a look at the method.

When a hesychast begins to pray, the first thing he does is to *relax*. "Hesychasm" comes from the Greek word for *rest*. He relaxes his body by assuming some posture that is both restful and reverent. The favorite posture is probably sitting, with the back and legs straight and the arms resting on the knees, palms of the hands upward. But one may stand or kneel, or even lie down, I suppose.

The hesychast relaxes his soul, too: this is a little harder to do, but it is even more important: to calm our emotions, to still our desires and cravings, and to silence all the noisy inward conversations and schemes and preoccupations of the mind. And he relaxes his *spirit*: that most inward part of his personality, his Self, where he will meet his God and be sanctified by Him. He does this by putting himself in the "lap of God" (Psalm 130), in silence and peace, in perfect trust.

REFLECTIONS ON THE JESUS PRAYER

That's the first step: to *relax*. As you can see, it's a life's work in itself. And the hesychast is not too discouraged if he doesn't succeed completely the very first time he tries. Nor does he wait for total success before passing on to the next step. A relative relaxation will do: just enough inward peace and silence so that he can pay *attention*. Attention to what? To his heart. He listens for his heart-beat. That's the second step: *Find the place of your heart.* And there is to be no cheating by taking your pulse. You must learn to sense your heart-beat *from inside*. (The whole hesychast spirituality is "from inside".) It is a drawing down of the mind from the head into the heart: concentrating, focusing, listening.

Listening to what? Here we come to the third step. And it is with this third step that the Prayer of the Heart really becomes a prayer. Because the hesychast is an Orthodox believer, he takes it for granted that God is *within* him. The Holy Trinity is *within* him. If the exterior world is a Temple, so is the interior world of his own body, his own personality. It is a Temple of the Holy Trinity. And it is such a Temple precisely in virtue of the Incarnation of the Second Person of that Trinity. The eternal Word of God took a body of the Blessed Virgin, died and rose gloriously on the Third Day in that same divinized body. And, because by baptism I became one with that body, and because by Holy Communion I am constantly sustaining that bodily oneness with Christ and growing in it—for these reasons, when I bring my mind down into my heart and listen, I discern not just my own heart-beat, but Christ's. It is because my body is Christ's body that I am a Temple. And my heart (His Heart) is the innermost sanctuary of that Temple. Therefore, when my mind is in my heart—and not only my mind, but my animal and vegetative drives and energies, too—then I am truly at prayer. For prayer is nothing else than attentiveness to God's presence. God is with us. "Let us be attentive," as we say in the Divine Liturgy.

If you never did anything else than these three steps, you would be a real hesychast, a real practitioner of the Prayer of the Heart. In fact, these three steps are the simplest and highest kind of prayer there can be, short of that God-given prayer of the Holy Spirit in us that comes only of His own special grace. But, as I said earlier, this "Prayer of the Heart" is not just a *method*. It is also a vocal prayer, with words; and it is a school of spirituality.

These first three steps that I have described, although a very good and complete form of prayer in themselves, are difficult. It is easy perhaps, in the flush of one's first enthusiasm, to feel a real success and joy in this discovery of God-within-us. But what do we do with the Prayer for the rest of our lives? It's a very rare soul indeed who can stay at this height of perception and warmth forever afterwards. Most of us soon fall back onto our own weakness, and are distracted by a million tendencies and emotions and thoughts. For us weaker brethren, there is a fourth step. And that is to use our heartbeat, once we have achieved enough peace to have discovered it, to address a short ejaculatory prayer to Jesus as present in our hearts. There are various prayers to Jesus that one could say. One could even make up or discover one's own. All that is possible within the hesychast tradition. But the time-honored version of it, the one which is found in the *Horologion* of our Church,[1] and the one which in fact most Orthodox Christians use, is the following:

"Lord Jesus Christ, Son of God,
Have mercy on me a sinner."

The heart becomes a kind of metronome (or drum, if you will) that beats out the rhythm, and the hesychast sets this little prayer in motion with the rhythm of his heart-beat, spacing it out any way that suits him best, as long as it is nice and slow, so

---

1. The *Horologion*, or Book of Hours, contains the unchangeable prayers of the Divine Office of the Orthodox Eastern Church. Some editions contain an admonition for the illiterate, the ill, and those traveling or otherwise prevented from attending the Hours of Prayer, to substitute the Jesus Prayer for the Hours missed. One is advised to repeat the Prayer 100 times as a substitute for Vespers, 50 times for Compline, 100 times for the Midnight Office, 300 times for Matins, 50 times for each of Prime, Terce, Sext and None, and 100 times for the Typika. The Jesus Prayer can thus be said to have attained a certain "official" status in the Church. It is used in this way by many of the monks of Mount Athos, for example.

that there's time for the prayer to "sink in."[2] And, like any musical rhythm, the last beat of the phrase leads on to the first beat of the next phrase: it is repeated over and over again—as long as we want to, as long as we can stand it, as long as we live, even. But for the Jesus Prayer to work, it must be genuine Prayer of the Heart: it must be said *attentively*. And it must be said in *peace* and with *faith*. It must be prayer not only of the body and of the mind, but it must be Prayer *from* the Heart. We must really *mean* it, be engaged in it, committed to it: body, soul, and spirit. Only such prayer is real prayer.

---

2. Many hesychasts also synchronize their breathing with the Prayer, repeating the first line as they inhale, the second line as they exhale. But this should only be done when one is quite relaxed and in good mental health. Such a complete psychosomatic technique ought not to be attempted without the guidance of a confessor or spiritual father who is himself experienced in the technique. The Jesus Prayer, when practiced in this way, begins to alter the psychic structure of the personality. Latent traumas, neurotic and psychotic tendencies may be yanked painfully to the surface of consciousness. Only use such a technique if a spiritual father of real discernment sees that this will be good for you. Spiritual pride or greed for "mystical" experiences can bring down a terrible punishment upon the soul that cannot abide humbly in God's will.

3. "Lord"

by calling upon the one God by His name, they could make Him present. Later, however, the Jewish religious minds developed such a deep reverence and awe for this powerful Name that they stopped pronouncing it. Only the High Priest ever pronounced it, and he only once a year, on the Day of Atonement, when he took the blood of the sacrificed animals into that innermost part of the Temple called the Holy of Holies. Otherwise, the Name of God was never spoken. When the Scriptures were read, or when the Psalms were sung, whenever God's Name came up in the text, they substituted the word *Lord:* Adonai. So that, in the Jewish mind, the word *Lord* had this mysterious and powerful connotation: it was connected with the unutterable Name of the Most High God. "Hear, O Israel, the *Lord* is our God, The *Lord* alone." This ancient Jewish invocation is, you might say, the Old Testament Gospel, the essential message. "The Lord is One, Holy, Mighty."

Now, when Jesus began His public ministry, no one knew Who He really was. "Is not this the carpenter's son, and is not his mother Mary, and do we not know his brothers and sisters?" Even his disciples considered Him as just a rabbi—a rabbi Who taught with amazing power and conviction, a rabbi Who healed the sick and drove out demons. But still, just a rabbi.

It wasn't until He rose on the Third Day that the truth hit them. It hit Mary Magdalene, as we have seen. It hit the disciples on their way to Emmaus, when Jesus blessed and broke the bread and gave it to them. It took Thomas a little longer: he doubted until he saw Jesus personally and put his hands into His wounds. But when the truth sank in, he made the classic expression of faith: "My Lord and my God!" No Jew ever used the word "Lord" lightly. When Thomas addresses Jesus in this way, he is bringing the whole Old Testament force of the word "Lord" to bear upon the situation. He is recognizing Jesus for what He really is: Adonai, the Lord, YHWH. "My *Lord* and my God" is a New Testament version of "Hear, O Israel, the *Lord* is our God the *Lord* alone." This is the Gospel, the Good

News. And the followers of Jesus had to wait until the Resurrection to hear it and understand it and believe it. Jesus had spoken to them of it before, but only now, as they saw Him gloriously risen, did they understand and *believe*. He is the *Lord*. When they see Him on the shores of Lake Galilee, after their night of fishing, they say: "It is the *Lord.*" The Lord is risen.

This title Lord is a proclamation, then, of Christ's Resurrection. It is a profession of faith in His Divinity. It is a proclamation of His power. He is the Lord, the only Lord, "You are our God, and we know no other."[2] "One is holy, one is *Lord*, Jesus Christ, unto the glory of God the Father. Amen."[3] He Is, He Who Is, He Who made the world, He Who made me, He Who brought Israel out of Egypt, He Who was born of Mary, He Who healed the sick, He Who heals me, He Who raised the dead, He Who

2. From Sunday Matins, hymn sung after the Resurrection Gospel.
3. From the Divine Liturgy, response sung after the Breaking of the Bread.

raises me every time I fall, He Who will raise me on the Last Day.

What happens inside me when I utter this powerful word "Lord"? If I say it with faith, if I say it *in* my heart and *from* my heart, He comes. The ancient pagan was right, in this much at least: when you call upon your God, He comes. Because when you address Jesus as Lord, you are making an act of faith in His Divinity. And an act of faith cleanses you of your sins and restores God's life in you. He-Who-Is now "Is" in you: He is creating your inner cosmos all anew, He is delivering you out of the Egypt of your own sinfulness, He is being born again in you, He is healing you, He is raising you up, *now*. St. Paul says, "If you confess with your lips that Jesus is *Lord* and believe in your *heart* that God raised him from the dead, you will be saved" (Rom 10:9). This confession of Jesus as *Lord*, this belief in the *heart* that He is risen from the dead, is essential to hesychast spirituality; it is essential to Eastern Christian piety; and it is essential to Christianity itself. This is the Good News.

4. Jesus

God has a first Name. The word "God," as you know, is not anybody's name. The pagans worship all sorts of gods and goddesses. "God" denotes a whole *class* of beings, just as "man" or "human" does. It doesn't connote a *person,* an *individuality.* It is the name that does that, always. We humans have names: a family name, a nationality (which is really a kind of name, too); maybe a patronymic: Petrovich, Petrovna, etc.;[1] but, most important of all, a *personal* name. The personal name is not where you come from or what you are, it is *who* you are. The first name is a mystery, because the human person is a mystery: immortal, individual, somebody to

1. Russians, Byelorussians and East Ukrainians use their fathers' Christian name as well as their own, adding the endings -ovich or -ovna (Ukrainian -ivna). Ivan Petrovich means "John, son of Peter"; Olga Petrovna would be "Olga, daughter of Peter." Then follows the family name. When a woman marries, she takes her husband's family name, but she keeps her patronymic (father's name). East Slavs thus go through life proclaiming both their identity and their paternity.

41

be known and *loved.* When people love each other, they call each other by their first names. If that love is very deep, sometimes that's all they say.

And so with God. When He revealed Himself to Moses, He told him He was the *only* God, and that Israel was to worship no other. But He also revealed His name. The Jews, however, through their religious fear, didn't use it. *Love* of God existed in Israel: if you pray the Psalms, you can't doubt it. But love did not predominate in the religion of Israel. The Jewish scruple at calling the Lord by His own Name is an expression of that. Fear, awe, reverence, predominated over love in the Old Testament. The word "Lord" (Adonai) was substituted for God's own Name, and it carried with it connotations of power, of holiness, and of high mystery. But not of love, particularly.

Now, when the archangel Gabriel came to Mary and announced the Good News of her conception, he also told her what her Child's name would be. "You will conceive in your womb and bear a son, and you shall call his name *Jesus*" (Lk 1:31). "For he will save his people from their sins" (Mt 1:21). *Jesus*, in Hebrew *Yehoshuah*, means "the Lord is salvation." And the name of this child was meant to reveal something of his personality and his destiny. To the Jewish mind, a name always did this, and Jewish parents never chose names for their children without a good deal of reflection and prayer: if the name *expressed* the destiny, it might also *make* the destiny of the child. Name-choosing was very important.

"Jesus" was a fairly common name for Jewish men: in a shortened Hebrew form, Joshua, it still is. (Our English and Slav forms, "Jesus" and "Isus," come from the Greek form of the name, "Iesous.") So when Jesus the carpenter of Nazareth began His public ministry, His name didn't strike his listeners as being unusual. Like so many other aspects of His personality and activity, it fitted into the Jewish way of life and its religious traditions. Everybody's name meant something religious, and many Jewish men were named "The-Lord-is-salvation." It was not until His followers got to know Him more intimately, and began little by little to realize that they were in the presence of something more than a Galilean Rabbi, something more even than a prophet—that they began to pay any attention to the homelier details of His personal life such as His Name, or His family tree, or His birthplace. And it was only with His resurrection that the full truth dawned upon them. His name was *Himself:* "The-Lord-is-salvation." "My Lord and my God," Thomas said. "Jesus, the Lord, is salvation." He is risen, and in rising has raised us from our sins. "Jesus" is not just a nice name that was given to a Jewish baby to place him under the Lord's saving protection. "Jesus" is what His Name says He is. "I am He-Who-Is," He had told Moses long ago. Now this Son of the Virgin stands among His disciples, gloriously risen, and says "I am salvation." *Yehoshuah*—Jesus.

And now man can call on his God by name again. For God is this man of Galilee, this Nazarene, and we know His Name—Jesus. And in this Name—a human name, a good, Jewish name—in this Name is all the power and the mystery and the awesomeness of the title Lord. This is the Name by which all men are saved, and without which no man can be saved. For this Jesus is indeed the only God there is. "You are our God, and we know no other."[2] "To all who received him, who believed in his *name,* he gave power to become children of God" (Jn 1:12). "God has highly exalted him and bestowed on him the *name* which is above every name, that at the *name* of Jesus every knee should bow, in heaven and on earth and under the earth, and every tongue confess that *Jesus Christ* is *Lord,* to the glory of God the Father" (Phil 2:9-11). "One is holy, one is Lord, Jesus Christ, unto the Glory of God the Father. Amen." "And there is salvation in no one else, for there is no other *name* under heaven given among men by which we must be saved" (Acts 4:12). "If you ask anything of the Father, he will give it to you in my *name* . . . ask, and you will receive, that your joy may be full" (Jn 16:23-24).

---

2. Sunday Matins, hymn to the risen Christ.

But, because *Jesus* is the name of a man, there is also a warmth and a familiarity and an accessibility about it. Among humans the name is an expression of love. And with the revelation of God in Jesus of Nazareth comes the revelation of Love. God is Love, the New Testament is the Testament of Love, Christianity is the religion of Love. We invoke the Name of our God, not just to make His power present in us, but because we *love* Him. When we pronounce the Name "Jesus," we are saved, not just through faith in Him (as with the title "Lord"); but we are saved by our love for Him. If we pray His Name *in* the heart, and *from* the heart, we are certainly in union with Him, in *love* with Him. "Jesus is Lord," "Lord, Jesus . . . " is the Good News not only of His Divinity; it is not only our profession of faith in Him; it is a declaration of our *love* for Him. And in this the whole of religion consists. Jesus is not just "Lord": He is *my* Lord, my Teacher, my Master. By the humanity He shares with me, He is my beloved Brother, my joy, my life.

Jesus, the Name that is above all names. Our

prayer life could consist of this Word alone. In fact, some Orthodox Christians use only this Word.[3] It is the central word of the Prayer, and of the whole Christian Mystery. In this Nazarene, this son of Mary, the Trinity have revealed Themselves to man: the Trinity and the whole depth and richness of God's plan for the universe, His unutterable love for men. Unutterable, yet uttered in the Word become flesh: Jesus.

God utters this Word to man. And we utter it, too, boldly and openly, with the boldness that comes of love, with the openness that comes of our secure consciousness of our brotherhood with Him, and of our sonship with His Father. Here is the real heart of hesychasm: warmth, affective piety, *immersion,* you might say, in the loving Presence of Jesus. It is not just the mind plunged into the heart. It is the whole personality immersed in the love of our Savior, Jesus. Immersed, at rest, secure. Love brings peace. *Hesychia.*

---

3. For a beautiful exposition of this form of the Jesus Prayer, cf. *The Prayer of Jesus,* by a monk of the Eastern Church, Desclée Company.

5. Christ

We usually think of "Christ" as being our Savior's name. It is so closely linked in Christian tradition with the name Jesus that it has become His "second name," so to speak: Jesus Christ. This usage goes back to St. Paul, and, among Eastern Christians, "Christ" is the commonest way of referring to the Savior, both in our liturgical prayers and in our everyday speech.

But "Christ," like "Lord," is a *title*, not a name. When we say "Jesus Christ," we really mean "Jesus *the* Christ." Jews in Jesus' time didn't have family names. They, like the modern Slavs, used their father's name: Simon son of Jonah, John son of Zebedee, James son of Alphaeus. Sometimes they acquired a nickname, indicating where they came from, or perhaps some personal characteristic that distinguished them: Joseph of Arimathea, Mary of Magdala, Simon the Zealot. And so with Jesus: He was known in His own town as Jesus son of Joseph. When His fame as a teacher and healer spread to other towns, people called Him "Jesus of Nazareth." We are not aware that He was ever nicknamed for any personal characteristic of His.

But the Gospels mention two people who perceived an extraordinary characteristic of His, and who named Him accordingly. His disciple Simon the Rock (i.e. Peter), in a moment of enthusiasm, said to Him: "You are the Christ, the son of the living God" (Mt 16:16). And His beloved friend Martha, mourning her brother's death and overjoyed and moved at Jesus' coming to comfort her and her sister Mary, made the same declaration: "I believe that you are the Christ, the Son of God" (Jn 11:27).

"You are *the* Christ." Who is *the* Christ? Or what is *a* Christ? What personal characteristic of our Savior does the word "Christ" reveal? Why did only two people, out of all His followers, ever apply this title to Him during His lifetime?

"Christ" is our English form of the Greek word "*Christós.*" It is the Greek equivalent of the

CHRIST

Hebrew title "Messiah." "Christ" and "Messiah" both mean, in their respective languages, "anointed." And it is to this idea of "anointing" that we must go if we are really to understand what a Christ is, what a Messiah is.

The word "anointing" doesn't mean much to the modern ear, apart from certain specialized religious meanings we give it. But if we go to the basic meaning of the word, we find that it is very simple: it's just a rubbing or spreading of some oily substance onto someone or something.

Now, what's so special about smearing oil on someone? Why should anyone who has had oil rubbed or poured on him (a "christ," in Greek) be set apart from anyone else? There is a mystery here, and it is hidden behind something very simple. But to understand this simplicity we must transport ourselves in space and time to another country and another society. It is a poor country, by our standards. There is not much fertile land, and most of that is cultivated to raise grain and vegetables and fruit-trees; the little grazing-land they do leave uncultivated feeds just enough cattle and sheep to give them milk and wool. Animals are not often slaughtered for food, and most people live on a vegetable diet. And when you subsist on grains and legumes, vegetable oil suddenly becomes an important commodity. It provides fat that your body needs—in fact, craves, if you are even slightly undernourished. It "dresses up" foods that otherwise would be very austere and tasteless. It makes salads possible—also the processes of baking and frying and roasting.

This society is also much less technologically advanced than our own. Petroleum is unknown—it is still locked tight in beds of rock thousands of feet underground, waiting for twentieth-century man to discover it. The only lubricant man has for his tools and simple machinery is the fats and oils that the vegetable kingdom can offer. They also provide fuel for his lamps.

The process of distillation has not yet been invented: alcohol and those other volatile liquids that can be made only through distilling are also

54

unknown. Thus, the only medium for preparing perfumes, medications and cosmetics is, again, oil.

Now, this country is on the eastern Mediterranean seaboard, and the olive tree grows well there. And the ripe fruit of the olive is a good source of oil. In autumn people go out with long canes to knock down the plump, black olives from the trees onto the ground. Then they gather them and take them to an olive press, often located right in the olive grove. There the press squeezes the olives into a thick oily paste which is then transferred to a cauldron of boiling water. The water cooks every last bit of oil out of the olive-pulp. Then the water is cooled. Pulp and pits sink to the bottom, and the wonderfully light, nut-fragrant golden-green oil rises to the surface. It is carefully poured off and stored in big earthenware jars, for it is precious stuff. This is the "oil of gladness" that turns a poor meal into a square meal, that makes light in the darkness, that softens rough and injured skin and sore muscles, that bears sweet-smelling herb-juices and powerful balms into the deep places of wounded and aching bodies, that can be imbued with perfumes for women—and for men, too—for feast-days and special occasions when we want to smell nice. And it's not something you waste or spill, because it takes a lot of olives—and a lot of hot, sweaty, dusty work—to make just a little oil.

Perfumed oil is especially precious. The Mediterranean climate grows a few sweet herbs and flowers to provide essences for perfume; but the best perfumes come from the tropical climate of "Sheba and Seba" in southern Arabia, and from certain islands to the south and east, in the Indian Ocean. Ships and caravans of camels bear these rare gums and spices thousands of miles before they reach the markets of Jerusalem or Damascus, and they are a very expensive commodity by the time they get there.

Such is oil. And in a sensitive, somewhat "primitive" society in which people's consciousness is not bombarded by heavy and indiscriminate unloadings of information, communications, philosophies, ideologies and noise—in such a society, oil, like every other living creature or inanimate object, is understood and perceived with a depth and an intensity we in our civilization rarely experience. So that when someone takes an alabaster jar, say, or a beautifully decorated ram's-horn full of rare, perfumed oil, and pours it on someone else's feet or his head, there is a very special significance in such an act. And it is done only to a very special person. When Moses consecrated the priests that God had set apart and indicated to him—Aaron and his sons—he prepared a special oil with precious perfumes, and he poured it on them, thereby instituting the priesthood and the cult of the Old Law (Lev 8). When the young man Saul was led by God's Holy Spirit into the household of Samuel (1 Sam 9 and 10), Samuel poured a "vial of oil" on his head, thereby instituting the office of kingship in Israel. And later, when Saul proved unworthy of his office, and Samuel went forth looking for a new king, he took with him a horn of oil. And when he arrived in Bethlehem, at the house of Jesse, and called forth Jesse's youngest son, David the Bethlehemite, from the sheepfold, he poured the oil on David, thereby establishing not only a new king, but a Royal Family that was to last forever, like the sun and the moon (Ps 88:37-38). David's son Solomon, and Solomon's son Rehoboam, and Rehoboam's son Abijam, and on down to Jehoiachin, the last king of David's line before the Babylonic captivity—all were anointed with the holy oil that was poured only on priests and kings. Every man whom God's Holy Spirit singled out from the ordinary crowd of men to rule over them, or to intercede for them before Him, was thus singled out and designated by the pouring of precious, fragrant oil on his head. Aaron and his sons, and the priestly line after him; and David and his sons, the kingly line—were "christs," "messiahs," anointed of the Lord, because the Spirit of God had come upon them, had given them a touch of Divinity.

With the "Babylonic captivity," the kingship was abolished, and Judah thereafter became a pawn in the struggle of rival imperial powers in the Middle East: first Babylon, then Persia, then the rival suc-

cessors of Alexander the Great, the Ptolemies of
Egypt and the Seleucids of Syria, then the Romans.
But down through these centuries of instability and
oppression, the Jews never forgot the glory of
David's sons. The Royal Family split up into
various collateral clans, all of them obscure, many of
them poor and proletarian. But the people kept hop-
ing that someday a Messiah, a Christ of David's
line, would again rule over them. And the Prophets
and the Psalms assured them that their hopes would
be fulfilled. The tree of Jesse would bloom again,
this time with a flower that would never fade, more
fragrant than all the oils and perfumes of Sheba and
Seba.

And so it came to pass. A young girl of one of the
poorest and most obscure offshoots of David's family, gave birth to a child in the family's ancestral city
of Bethlehem in Judah. His birth was announced
to some local shepherds by an angel who called
the Child "a Savior, (the) Christ the Lord" (Lk 2:11).
The last and long-awaited "anointed" of David's
line had come. And He is both "anointed" (that is,

king) and *Lord*. This Christ, son of David, has more than a touch of Divinity to Him. He is the Lord.

Jesus, like Aaron and the priests, and like His illustrious forefather David, was singled out from the ordinary crowd of men by an anointing. Like Saul and David, He was designated by the Spirit of God. The sweet perfume of the Holy Spirit filled the virginal womb of His mother, and by that act of the Father's Power, so mighty and yet so tender, she conceived His Son. This last of the Kings and Priests was christed with the Chrism of God's very nature and substance. This Christ is the Lord.

During Jesus' lifetime He kept this secret of His Christhood carefully to Himself. His consciousness of it seems to have deepened suddenly at two critical points in His life: at His Baptism and at His Transfiguration. When John baptized Him in the waters of the Jordan, the Spirit came upon Jesus with a power and an insistence He had not known since His mother's womb. And His mind opened (as a man's mind will, when he reaches the age of thirty) to a new intuition of Himself, and His ears opened to

the call of the Spirit. He put aside His carpenters'
tools and began to do that which He was sent to do:

> *"The Spirit of the Lord is upon me, because he
> has anointed me to preach good news to the
> poor" (Lk 4:18).*

Again at His Transfiguration on Mount Tabor,
the Spirit erupted from within Him in a dazzling
light, and again His ears were opened to the voice of
God. And in this overwhelming experience of the
Father's love for Him, His mind again opened to a
new intuition of His Christhood: He now understood
that He was a priest, and that He had been anointed
to offer sacrifice in Jerusalem. "The Son of man will
be delivered into the hands of men, and they will kill
him; and when he is killed, after three days he will
rise" (Mk 9:31).

But after this new Passover had been sacrificed,
Jesus' secret, which hitherto had been guessed only
by two other people, was suddenly poured out. The
Spirit erupted from within Him again in an over-

whelming wave of energy that raised Him from the dead, and poured out of His Body into the bodies of others, so that their minds and eyes and ears were opened to know Who and What He is. The flood of this Chrism broke upon the myrrh-bearing women and then on the other disciples; and on the Fiftieth Day of this new and never-ending Feast, with a new surge of power It loosed the tongues of men and filled every corner of the earth. With this Chrism we are henceforth all christed. To as many as believe in His Name, He has given the power to become sons of God. We are His good odor, and we fill His Temple with our fragrance (His fragrance). We are kings and priests, set aside to rule and to offer sacrifice.

There are many ways in which we offer sacrifice, but preeminently we offer it when we pray. The Prayer of the Heart is a sacrifice of the heart. Anointed with the Chrism of Jesus, we stand in this inner sanctuary, before this altar, and breathing deeply we call the Spirit down on to the Holy Gifts there set forth. And because we are priests, He comes. He transforms the Gifts into Him Who is

CHRIST

Priest and Gift and God, all in one. This Inner
Liturgy is offered with every heart-beat and every
breath, and it exhales the good odor of Christ up to
the Father, and into the nostrils of every other wor-
shiper in this vast Temple which is not just cosmos,[1]
but Communion of Saints and Church.

You begin to see, I hope, that the Jesus Prayer is
not just an announcing of the Gospel. It is an *enact-
ment* of it: as the Prayer takes root in our hearts, it
begins to change our personalities. It is no longer I
who live, but Christ lives in me, and I begin to live
out the Gospel. The same things that happened to
Jesus begin to happen to me: He is born in me, He
grows in me, He teaches in me, He heals in me, He
suffers in me, dies in me, rises in me, pours His
Spirit into me and into others through me; and all
this not through external activity or through
brilliant insights or strong emotional experiences of
God's love for us and our love for Him—but simply
by beating our hearts and breathing: by *being*.
These basic rhythms of our bodies beat out the ac-

---

1. Cf. Section One on the cosmic Temple.

cents of the Divine Liturgy. The murmuring streams of blood and breath sing the praises of the All-Holy Trinity. And all this happens because Jesus is the Christ, and we are christed with His Chrism.

6. Son of God

The central fact, the "Good News" of our faith, is that Jesus is God. The titles "Lord" and "Christ" both say that, though in very different ways. And in the title "Christ," as we have seen, the mystery of Jesus' personality is linked with us, His followers, in a special way. For to be a "Christ" is an essentially human thing; and, like all human things, it is involved with the rest of material creation. A christ is a *man*: a special man, to be sure, one who is singled out from the others; but a man, all the same, with a human body upon which the fruit of the earth, oil and spices and perfumes, can be poured; a man endowed with specifically human gifts of insight, strength of character, leadership, attractiveness of personality, and that self-sacrificing generosity that distinguishes a great leader from a demagogue or a dictator; a christ is a man *of* the people and *for* the people. He is both leader and servant. A king is always in some way a servant; a priest is always in some way a victim.

And so with Jesus. He is a villager of Nazareth, a carpenter, a subject and tax-payer of Caesar. More important, He is "son of Joseph," son of Mary, of the family of David, of the tribe of Judah, of the nation of Israel. He, too, is endowed with human qualities that fit Him for a special mission and destiny. He is a teacher and a healer, and a man of great love and compassion Who attracts people to Himself, especially the unfortunate and the downtrodden, and children. He has a commanding personality that makes His followers want to put Him on the throne of Israel. He is a man of sufficient courage to die for His convictions.

But He is more than that. His humanity has been singled out for something more momentous than to teach a new ethical doctrine; He is more than a faith healer, more than a compassionate friend of the people, more than a martyr. He is a Victim. "Destroy this Temple, and in three days I will raise it up" (Jn 2:19). The Temple of which He speaks is His own

Body, out of which rivers of living water will flow, which will be "food indeed and drink indeed" (Jn 6:55) for those who eat and drink of this Passover sacrifice. It is not for any one human gift that He has been singled out by God. His entire humanity has been set apart, consecrated, "anointed": the body that was formed in His mother's womb, built and knit together by "her own pure blood" as our hymns often say, nourished by the bread and wine and oil of Palestinian soil; the mind and temperament and personality that He inherited from His family and that was formed by His environment; the whole living soul and spirit that was Jesus of Nazareth: this is what God set aside.

Why? What made this man so special as to be called to such a unique role: to be Victim, to be source of life to the rest of His fellow-men? How can any mere man be living bread, so that when we eat of it we shall live forever? Is this not Jesus, the son of Joseph, whose father and mother we know? (Jn 6:42).

But who, in fact, is His father? Do we really know? Joseph brought him up, supported him,

taught him a trade, and perhaps was in turn supported by him before he died. But who begot him?
There is a mystery in Jesus' life, a secret. "You do
not know where I come from," he tells his adver-
saries (Jn 8:14). Flesh and blood cannot discern this
mystery. Flesh and blood can pry out a scandal, or
speculate tantalizingly on certain things in Jesus'
family background that "don't fit together." But
the story of Jesus' conception and birth is not that
kind of a secret. It is a "mystery hidden from the
ages and unknown to angels," as one of our hymns
says.[1] Mary withheld the identity of Jesus' real
father not because it was scandalous but because it
was a mystery. Jesus' time had not yet come. His
mother must keep these things in her heart (Lk
2:51), she must not yet reveal Who He is. People
would mock her and her Child. "Do not give what is
holy to dogs" (Mt 7:6). The secret is kept until Jesus
is a grown man, nearing the end of His life. And
when He proclaims the identity of His Father, it
does in fact create a scandal, though not of the kind

---

1. Resurrectional Theotokion, Mode 4.

70

that such a revelation can usually be expected to cause. The scandal does not lie in a disclosure that some man other than Joseph, His mother's husband, fathered Him. The terrible stumbling-block of Jesus' self-revelation lies in the fact that His Father is God, the Lord. "You are from below," He tells the skeptics, "but I am from above" (Jn 8:23). "I have come in my Father's name" (Jn 5:43) ". . . the Father who sent me bears witness to me" (Jn 8:18). Such language horrified and angered the majority of the Jewish leaders who heard it. It was blasphemy. So they ". . . sought to kill him, because he . . . called God his Father, making himself equal with God" (Jn 5:18).

And when He came to Jerusalem to celebrate the Passover, they did kill Him. He was put on trial before the High Priest and sentenced to death for His abominable claims. "What further testimony do we need? We have heard it ourselves from his own lips?" (Lk 22:71). The scandal of Jesus' paternity was too great for the people to bear. He must be crucified.

REFLECTIONS ON THE JESUS PRAYER

Jesus died precisely to bear witness to the true identity of His Father. And His death did in fact reveal His Sonship. "This was indeed the Son of God," exclaimed the Roman centurion who superintended Jesus' execution (Mt 27:54). And on the third day, Jesus' body was filled with the Holy Spirit which His Father breathed into it. And when this new Adam rose again out of the earth from which He was made, it was apparent to all who saw Him that He is the Son of God. "I and the Father are one," He had told them (Jn 10:30). Now they understood. "My Lord and my God." As the Father is Lord (YHWH) so the Son is Lord (YHWH). Come, let us worship the Lord. Jesus' resurrection from the dead, with the out-pouring of His Holy Spirit into those who saw Him, was the cause and beginning of their faith. It was in seeing Him, in realizing Who-He-Is, that they were saved. This realization of His identity, of His Sonship, is the cause of life in those who see and believe. The phrase "Son of God," like the first three invocations in the Jesus Prayer, leads us to the heart of the Gospel.

SON OF GOD

The Gospel message is that Jesus is the Son of God. The apostles, filled and vivified with this Good News, this faith, went forth and told the rest of the world. For it is only by faith that Jesus is the Son of God that man can live. Without this faith life is impossible. "The life I now live in the flesh I live by faith in the Son of God," says St. Paul joyfully (Gal 2:20). This is the whole summary of his message and his life work. Everywhere he went, he "proclaimed Jesus, saying 'He is the Son of God' " (Acts 9:20). "This book was written," says another apostle, "that you may believe that *Jesus* is the *Christ,* the *Son of God,* and that believing you may have life in his name" (Jn 20:31). This, then, is the essence of the Christian message: that Jesus is the Christ, the Son of God. This message, heard and accepted and carried in the heart, empowers us to live forever.

Everyone who carries this message in his heart is born again of the same Father Who begot Jesus. We, too, are His sons and daughters. And this new life which we now bear within us will not die. "Whoever lives and believes in me shall never die"

REFLECTIONS ON THE JESUS PRAYER

(Jn 11:26). "This is the will of my Father, that every one who sees the Son and believes in him should have eternal life; and I will raise him up at the last day" (Jn 6:40). Born of God, we shall overcome the world: all our sorrows, all that threatens us, hurts us, betrays us, wrongs us, sickens us, kills us: we shall overcome it. "Whatever is born of God overcomes the world . . . and who is it that overcomes the world but he who believes that Jesus is the Son of God?" (1 Jn 5:4-5). This is our victory, our faith: Jesus the Son of God.

As the hesychast lives and breathes, his heartbeat proclaims this powerful and life-giving message constantly, day and night. The unceasing rhythms of his life-organs drum it deeper and deeper into his soul. And if he can surrender to it and live it, then the fruits of this proclamation will be very rich indeed. His own sonship with the Father will grow constantly more intimate, his own identity with the Son will grow ever more apparent to others—and even to himself—as he lives out the life of Christ in his own person. And his infusion with, and possession by, the Holy Spirit, will become more and more complete. He will be progressively "divinized," as the Fathers like to put it, until he reaches that point of Passover from life to death to new life, when the flesh of the old Adam is burned completely away, and nothing is left but the new Man, raised gloriously from the clay by the power of the Spirit Whom the Father breathes into Him. Dying, he shall die no more. Living, he shall live forever.

"Rabbi, thou art the Son of God, thou art the King of Israel."

"Because I said to you, I saw you under the fig tree, do you believe? You shall see greater things than these . . . Truly, truly, I say to you, you will see heaven opened, and the angels of God ascending and descending upon the Son of man" (Jn 1:49-51).

7. Have Mercy On Me

As he drew near to Jericho, a blind man was sitting by the roadside begging; and hearing a multitude going by, he inquired what this meant. They told him, "Jesus of Nazareth is passing by." And he cried, "Jesus, Son of David, have mercy on me!" (Lk 18:35-38).

And as he entered a village, he was met by ten lepers, who stood at a distance and lifted up their voices and said, "Jesus, Master, have mercy on us" (Lk 17:12-13).

But the tax collector, standing far off, would not even lift his eyes to heaven, but beat his breast, saying, "God, be merciful to me a sinner!" (Lk 18:13).

The Good News, as we have seen, is the proclamation that Jesus is Lord and Christ and Son of God. But it is something more than a proclamation—or, rather, it is a proclamation that has an effect. It is not for the mind only, to learn and assent to. The Good News heals. It forgives. It reconciles. It sets things right: broken hearts, twisted bodies, tormented souls. "The blind receive their sight and the lame walk, lepers are cleansed and the deaf hear, and the dead are raised up, and the poor have good news preached to them" (Mt 11:5). The Good News is salvation. The Son of God *saves:* Yehoshuah, "the Lord is Salvation." Jesus' very name has power. "In the name of Jesus Christ of Nazareth, walk," Peter commands the lame man in the Temple. "And leaping up he stood and walked" (Acts 3: 6, 8).

The Gospel heals. In the Eastern Church we read it over the sick. In the Sacrament of Anointing we actually place the open book, words facing downward, over the head of the sick person. The Word of God has such power to heal. We read It over those who are troubled or afflicted in spirit, whether by their own personalities or by other spirits. The Gospel drives out unclean and troublesome spirits. When the Gospel is sung during Matins or the Divine Liturgy, people sometimes come and kneel or prostrate themselves beneath the Book while the holy words are being proclaimed: the sick come, the troubled come, those seeking some special blessing or favor; women come with their babies in their arms, or in their wombs. The Good News heals. Never imagine, O Christian, that the Gospel is just doctrine. It has power. And those who are humble enough to come forward and receive this Word in their hearts with faith, will feel that power. "Your faith has made you well," Jesus says repeatedly to those whom He has healed.

There must be faith, there must be humility. The Gospel is not magic. It is not some abracadabra that can be gabbled over some one who has been dragged willy-nilly beneath the book. The sick man must step forward of his own free will. He must know that he is sick, he must *desire* to be healed, and he must believe that Jesus is the Son of God, "Yehoshuah—the-Lord-is-Salvation." He must step forth out of the crowd, hobbling if he is lame, groping if he is blind, stinking and shunned if he is a

81

leper. He must cry out, "Jesus, Son of God, have mercy on me!" He must be ready even to grovel, as the Canaanite woman groveled on behalf of her little girl. "Even the dogs eat the crumbs that fall from their master's table" (Mt 15:27).

There must be humility, and an intense desire to be healed, a desire that overcomes our reticence, our self-sufficiency, our false sense of dignity. We must be aware of our helplessness. Only if we can face our own emptiness will we be able to make the humble pilgrimage to Jesus. Humility is the foundation of faith, and the external manifestation of it. Those who preferred the anonymity of the crowd to self-exposure were not healed. Those who maintained the splendid isolation of their social positions were not saved. It was the Canaanites (Mt 15:21-29), the Jairuses (Mk 5:22), the centurions (Mt 8:5-13) who were saved: those who lowered themselves to seek help of this Galilean carpenter. Jesus "*saw* their faith," the Gospel says repeatedly. He saw it in the humility that brought them to Him. And their faith "made them well."

HAVE MERCY ON ME

It always hurts a little to make this humble pilgrimage. Sometimes it hurts intensely. For those who are very proud, it is only the paroxysm of extreme anguish that will drive them to throw themselves at the feet of Jesus, to prostrate themselves beneath the Gospels in the sight of the congregation. There must be a "little death," an "inner martyrdom," as the hesychasts call it. "Give blood, receive the Spirit."[1] We must empty ourselves in order to be filled with God.

Many of the hesychast masters (or *startzy,* to use the Slav word) warn the beginner that at first the Jesus Prayer may be repugnant, or that it may even cause pain. There are perhaps several reasons why the Jesus Prayer can cause pain, but one of them is contained in the phrase "have mercy on me." It is a humbling phrase, a phrase that tests our faith. Before this utterance can come from the heart, we must know that we are sick, and we must desire to be healed. We must face our deformities, our

---

1. A much-quoted maxim in the spirituality of the Eastern Fathers.

ugliness, our stench, our abandonment. This is not always easy. In fact, at the outset, we may not be very much aware of our sickness. One of the preliminary effects of the Prayer as it begins to work its way into the depths of the personality will be to illumine the darkness there. And what we see under that light may upset us. The Prayer probes the depths of the psyche. Its rays search out our defects, our wounds, our sins, our memories. That is why, among other reasons, the Fathers insist that the beginner have a guide. For the Jesus Prayer not only probes, it does surgery, it sometimes cauterizes—the old Adam must be burned away. And burning hurts. We need guidance, reassurance, the experience of someone who has lived through these things, who can strengthen our faith and our hope. We need to know that the pain of seeing our own ugliness is life-giving, that it is the Holy Spirit already groaning within us (Rom 8:26), driving us out of the anonymous crowd and impelling us toward the feet of Jesus. We need to know that this surgery is bringing healing, that as the old Adam is burned away, the New Man is being born in us.

For the Jesus Prayer is the Gospel. And the Gospel has power. Never imagine, O hesychast, that the Jesus Prayer is just words. Once you begin to pray these words "from the heart," in the hesychast meaning of that phrase, you have introduced the Word of God into the deep places of your psyche. And the Word of God is sharper than any two-edged sword, piercing to the division of soul and spirit, of joints and marrow, and discerning the thoughts and intentions of the heart (Heb 4:12). It will reveal you to yourself as you never knew yourself before. And it will heal you. For the Jesus Prayer is the Gospel, and the Gospel heals.

So be of good courage. If you ask for mercy, you shall receive mercy. And what is mercy? Mercy is not just some petty concession made grudgingly by a worldly potentate to those wretched underlings whom his personal whim moves him to spare. The language of this world has thus cheapened the word "mercy." But what is mercy in the language of the

REFLECTIONS ON THE JESUS PRAYER

Kingdom? Mercy is the oil of God,[2] poured into our wounds, nourishing our bodies, lighting the lamps of our souls, making the wheels of the universe go round. Mercy is the Omnipotence of God. Nothing can go so wrong that God cannot set it right. No one can get so sick that God cannot heal him. Mercy is the power of God. Mercy is one of the Divine Energies,[3] working mightily in His creation and manifesting Him, making Him visible and known. When we experience this mercy, we know Who He Is. Our eyes are opened, and we see Him. We were blind from birth, and we didn't know it. And when

---

2. In Greek, the words "mercy" *(eleos)* and "oil" *(elaion)* are similar enough to make a pun on them. This "holy pun" occurs occasionally in our hymnody.

3. In Eastern Christian theological language the Divine Energies are God's manifestations of Himself in the universe, as distinguished from God's inner Trinitarian life. The teaching of the Fathers is that each Energy not only manifests God: it *is* God, the Holy Trinity appearing and acting through and in Creation though distinct from it. Some of the Energies are: Wisdom, Power, Love, Mercy, Anger (the "wrath of God"), Grace, Light (the "Uncreated Light"), Justice, Judgment, Fire, Beauty (i.e. God's own beauty, not created beauty), Silence, Mind, Holy of Holies, Goodness, Truth. It is said that if the names of all the Divine Energies were written down, the entire cosmos could not hold the books that would be necessary in order to "index" them.

we found out, one terrible day, we agonized in our darkness. But, impelled by the unutterable groanings of the Spirit, we stumbled forward, groping for the Light. "Jesus, Son of David, have mercy on me!" (Mk 10:47). And the Son of God, in His great power, gave us this mercy for which we asked. He spat on the ground and made clay of the spittle (Jn 9:6) and anointed our eyes with the oil of His mercy, and bade us wash in the pool of His mercy. So we went, and we washed, and we received our sight. And when our eyes were opened, we knew Who He Is, and seeing, we believed.

"Do you believe in the Son of man?"
"And who is he, sir, that I may believe in him?"
"You have seen him, and it is he who speaks to you."
He said, "Lord, I believe"; and he worshiped him (Jn 9).

87

8. Of Sin And Sinners

The great English historian Arnold Toynbee suggests that one of the serious shortcomings of Western civilization is its loss of the sense of *sin*.[1] The very word "sin," he remarks, if mentioned in serious academic circles, makes the agnostic or "liberal" intellectual "see red." He considers the implications of this attitude important enough to devote a section of his monumental *Study of History* to it.[2] The notion of sin, according to Professor Toynbee, implies the notion of personal responsibility, and the notion of responsibility implies the notion of freedom. To reduce this line of reasoning to its simplest terms, if you are capable of *sin*, that is because you are *free*.

As long as a society is growing and healthy and robust, Toynbee goes on (and what he says of a

1. Toynbee, Arnold, *A Study of History*, vol. V, p. 439.
2. Vol. V, pp. 432-439.

society can, I think, be applied to an individual), it retains a confidence in its freedom, in its ability to direct its own affairs and determine its own destiny, for good or for bad. But when a civilization "breaks down" (to use a technical expression of his), when things begin to go badly, there are three possible ways in which it can react. It can explain its predicament in terms of *fatalism,* of *drift,* or of *sin.* *Fatalism* is the idea that it doesn't matter much what we do, it's all been pre-determined, and we are mere pawns in a vast, impersonal game. *Drift* is the lack of any sense of direction at all: life is essentially absurd, meaningless, "one damned thing after another," to quote a schoolboys' humorous definition of history; nothing matters. *Fatalism* and the sense of *drift* both reject the notion of human freedom, and both are ominously present in our culture.

But there is a third reaction which a society (or an individual) can have with respect to its own "breakdown" or failure, and it is to this that we shall devote this final section on the Jesus Prayer. This

92

third reaction is to see break-down and failure, whether collective or individual, in terms of *sin.* It is this reaction which the Old Testament prophets preached to Israel in its break-down, and which is a permanent and indispensable feature of any genuine Christian spirituality. "We have sinned against the Lord our God, we and our fathers" (Jer 3:25). Unlike the sense of fate and the sense of drift, the sense of sin presupposes that man is free, and that he is the creature of a personal God Who is also free. In fact, it is precisely in our freedom that we resemble our God. "Let us make man in our image, after our likeness," the Holy Trinity deliberated among Themselves in the beginning (Gn 1:26). And so They freely made a free creature who, by his freedom, was to bring the rest of creation, tilled and tamed and subdued, and offer it back to Them as a sacrifice of praise.[3]

But because man was free, he didn't *have* to live up to the Holy Trinity's loving expectations. He

3. It is to this wider, fuller offering that the Divine Liturgy points when it speaks of the Eucharist as a "sacrifice of praise."

could choose his own line of action. And he did so. Adam did so, and "died the death" (Gn 2: 17). Israel did so, and was carried captive to Babylon. Every time we choose self instead of God, there is some sort of a "break-down." One of the uses to which we can put our God-given freedom is to throw it away and get ourselves carried captive into some predicament. But if we carry into our captivity some memory of our former freedom, then we will be able to say with Israel, "We have sinned"—i.e., "we could have done otherwise. This didn't *have* to happen. It was not predestined by an impersonal Fate, nor is it an absurd and meaningless catastrophe. It happened because we chose to do things our way instead of God's way." All this is implied in the classic Jewish and Christian phrase "We have sinned."

If man in his captivity can bring himself to utter this phrase, well and good. This is an admission of guilt, and a sense of guilt—that is, a sense of personal responsibility for sin—is the first necessary step towards release from captivity. "I confess that I am guilty," sings the Psalmist, "and my sin fills

me with dismay" (Ps 37:19). But it is only the first
step. Dismay is not a very nourishing food,
spiritually. Guilt without release is a living death.
"The very commandment which promised life proved
to be death to me," complains St. Paul of a religious tradition which awakened the sense of sin
in man without providing the means of release from
it (Rom 7:10). And our Western society, having jet-
tisoned the notion of sin, has been unable to release
its children from the guilt of sin. The intellect may
reject the theological concept, but the deeper levels
of the psyche have a gnawing sense of wrong. Guilt
without a sense of compunction, of repentance, of
release, is not merely deadening, it is maddening,
and our mental institutions and our psychiatrists'
waiting-rooms are full of people who no longer
believe in sin, but who are crushed with guilt. Our
new, post-Christian "sinless society" is as impotent
to deliver man from his bondage as was the old,
pre-Christian dispensation of Law of which St. Paul
complained. "Who will deliver me from this body of
death?" cries the Apostle (Rom 7:24). That is what

the mental patients and the drug-addicts and the alcoholics are crying. "Who will deliver me from my bondage?" And that is what you and I have cried, O Christian, in the time of our own "break-down" in the days before we knew Christ, and still do cry in our lesser daily break-downs and failures. "There is no man living who does not sin," says the great prayer for the dead, "O God of Spirits," which we repeat so often at funerals and memorial services.

There is no man living who does not sin. Sin is a lamentable fact of life—of that life in the flesh, that "body of death" in which we are still struggling, in which we are still making our clumsy attempts to be free. As long as we are honest and humble, we will be forced to admit that these attempts are not always successful. The man who refuses to admit his sinfulness is a liar. We have all tried to place our hope in our own righteousness, and it matters very little whether we have done so in the Old Testament manner, by trusting in external deeds and observances, or in the "post-Christian" manner, by rejecting the very notion of sin as degrading and "negative." Our own efforts to justify ourselves can never work. All our good works, all our philanthropy, all our "political involvement," all the power of our "positive thinking," cannot lift us up out of our sin, cannot deliver us from the bondage of our guilt. There is only one Who can set us free, and that is Jesus, the Son of God. The free God Who created us free, of His own free and loving will became man for us, emptied Himself for us (Ph 2:7), was made to be sin for us (2 Cor 5:21), nailed our flesh to the Cross, and with it nailed the curse of our guilt (Col 2:14), dying once and for all that we might live (Rom 6:10); through the power of His Holy Spirit, His Father raised Him up on the third day, and in His gloriously risen and Spirit-filled Body He delivers us from the "body of our death." When I cry out, "Who will deliver me from this death?" this is His answer, as He stands glorified at the mouth of my tomb: "Come forth unto resurrection."[4] "All things have been delivered into My hands, and I deliver you from sin, from guilt, from sickness, from suffering,

4. Resurrectional Kontakion, mode 7.

from death and stench and the grave. Come forth, Lazarus, from your captivity (Jn 11:43); 'come forth, prisoner, from your darkness.' "[5]

And I, even in my captivity, am still free. Under the dirt of my sins I still bear the image and likeness of my Creator. I don't have to wallow helplessly and hopelessly. If I was free to sin, I am also free to repent. It's so simple. I have only to reach out my hand from my grave, from my coffin, from the body of my death, and the Life-Giver will lift me up. With one powerful pull, the Mighty One will lead me out into the endless dance of that Easter Day which knows no evening.[6] He and I and Adam and Eve and all our beloved ones will beat the rhythm of that dance "with happy feet"[7] upon the resounding green meadows of Paradise.

So please understand, O Christian, that the words "sin" and "sinner" are not negative. They are only the reverse side of the coin of our freedom, and this

5. 2nd sticheron at Saturday Vespers, Mode 5. Cf. Is 49:9.
6. 4th sticheron at Saturday Vespers, mode 5.
7. Easter Canon of St. John Damascene, Ode 5, Stanza 2.

coin is stamped with the image and likeness of God. Hesychast spirituality, like all Eastern Christian spirituality, is acutely conscious of sin. But it is so only because our spirituality is so very conscious of freedom. God has set before us a momentous choice. That we have such a choice is our great glory. That we abuse that choice through sin is our great shame. But there could be no shame if it weren't for the glory. Christ is risen, and because we are free to choose the risen Christ, there is no need to remain in our shame. We can choose the glory. God grant us always to choose the glory.

The Jesus Prayer does not end with the word "sinner," for the simple reason that the Jesus Prayer does not end at all. "Sinner" is the last word of our exhalation. It empties our lungs. And as we begin to fill them again with our next breath, the heartbeat, starting with "Lord," begins to beat out the Good News once more. As in a musical rhythm, the last weak beat in the measure serves as the springboard to the strong first beat of the next measure.

REFLECTIONS ON THE JESUS PRAYER

"Sinner" is the weak beat that leads us to "Lord,"
and the Lord is our strong beat.

And so the dance goes on.

Appendix: What To Read

Not all hesychasts read. Many in past ages have been illiterate. Those advanced in prayer (usually in old age) need no further "information" than what the Prayer, activated by the Holy Spirit, pours into them. But there is a tradition of reading among Eastern Christian monks, and hesychasts through the ages have been formed by it. It is all very good stuff, and as appropriate and "relevant" today as it ever was.

First, the Holy Gospels. There is a wonderful interrelation between the Gospels and the Jesus Prayer. The Gospels feed the Prayer, and the Prayer opens the ears ever wider to the depths of meaning in the Gospels. Read the four Gospels through from beginning to end, then start over. This is a lifetime reading program. Read a little each day. Just a few verses read "from the heart" is sufficient. There is no hurry to finish a Book with which you are never going to be finished. Live with it. In time, its words and phrases, its very way of thinking, will become your own. This will help you to acquire the "mind of Christ."

Next, the Epistles of St. Paul. For these, it helps very much to have an annotated edition of the Bible. There are many things in St. Paul which are "hard to understand," as St. Peter rightly observes (2 Peter 3:16), and a good commentary by some reliable Orthodox or Roman Catholic theologian will be helpful. St. Paul's Epistles are themselves such a fine commentary on the Gospels that it is well worth the mental effort required to thread one's way through the argumentations of this great rabbinical mind. To those who say, "I'm not intelligent enough to understand St. Paul," I say: trust the Holy Spirit to help you.

Read also the three little Epistles of St. John, the "beloved disciple"—the Theologian, as we call him. (This, I think, is the meaning of the title "Divine" that he gets in the King James translation of the Bible.)

APPENDIX: WHAT TO READ

Read the Psalms, the Prayer Book of the Church. Read them according to any plan you wish: one of the great liturgical traditions—Anglican, Roman, Byzantine, or other—or according to some simpler and more spontaneous system of your own. For the beginner, and even for the more experienced, some kind of structured, formal prayer is very helpful, and the Psalms are the backbone of the formal prayer services of all the great Christian liturgical traditions. If you read the Psalms "from the heart" often enough so that their words and phrases, their feelings and aspirations, become your own, you will have been schooled very well in the art and science of prayer.

Read the rest of the Bible. Good notes by trustworthy orthodox theologians help. *Never confine your Bible reading to your "favorite passages."* You will end up fashioning a private "revelation" and a private "spirituality." Such a revelation, such a spirituality, cannot be authentic. Read the whole Bible, even the boring or vindictive or violent passages. To those who say, "I can't understand this, I can't accept that," I say: trust the Holy Spirit to help you. You must be a Christian of the Church, and the Bible is at the same time the Church's most inspired literary production and her most precious source of written Tradition. It cannot be ignored, either in whole or in part. Read it according to any plan you like, at any speed you like. But read it all.

Those who are members of one of the Orthodox or "Uniate" Catholic Churches may have access to the hymnody of the Byzantine Rite, whether through participation in daily Matins and Vespers in some church or monastery that offers them to the public, or through private reading or singing from our liturgical books. We regard our hymnody as far more than merely the "propers" of an ecclesiastical "rite." The Eastern Orthodox Church ranks its vast repertoire of liturgical hymns and prayers as one of the fountains of Orthodoxy, along with the Bible, the Ecumenical Councils and the Fathers. The Christian who knows and can sing "from the heart" the hymns of our Church has received a far better

APPENDIX: WHAT TO READ

theological training than any academic course of studies alone can give. And those of you who want to understand better our ascetical tradition, whether hesychasm exclusively, or the wider tradition of which it is a part, will find the liturgical poetry of our Church an excellent background and key to the rich mystical and ascetical literature of our Apostolic Churches of the East. More than that, the hymnody of our offices teaches you how to pray. The Psalms, the backbone of our Church Offices, school you in that universal art and science of prayer which is shared by all the Church of Christ. The hymnody introduces you to that particular style and modality of this art and this science that has produced the spirituality of the Christian East.

Read the Fathers. The Fathers, like the liturgical prayer of the Church, are a continuity of that perfect Revelation which is the Bible. Holy Tradition speaks through them, as it does through the Bible or through the hymnody. The Fathers, of course, constitute a vast literature: the famous collection of Migne runs to almost four hundred large, heavy volumes, and that is only the Latin and Greek Fathers. The Syriac, Coptic, Armenian, Ethiopian, Georgian, Slavonic and modern Russian and Arabic writings that are recognized as authentic expressions of Holy Tradition make the literature vaster still. Where does one begin?

The time-honored solution to this problem is the anthology. Since early monasic times collections of favorite writings have been made: *Paterika* ("Father" books) and *Philokalias* ("*philokalia*" means "love of beauty") of various sorts. The most widely used *Philokalia,* which has become for hesychasts the *Philokalia par excellence,* is one compiled by two monks of Mount Athos in the eighteenth century and published in Greek in 1782. It became the basic textbook of the hesychast revival that spread from Greece to the Slav countries and brought about the wonderful modern flowering of hesychasm in nineteenth and twentieth century Russia. The collection was enlarged and translated into Church Slavonic. That translation was then translated into Russian, and much of that Russian translation has subsequently been translated into English through the diligence and dedication of E. Kadloubovsky and G.E.H. Palmer. A new English translation is being prepared direct from the Greek by Father Kallistos Ware, an Orthodox priest and scholar of Oxford, England, who is also a monk of the Monastery of Patmos, Greece. To my knowledge, Father Kallistos' translation has not yet appeared.

The *Philokalia* is basic reading for the hesychast, and it is essential for anyone who wishes to learn what the Jesus Prayer really is, and what hesychasm really is. It is especially important for those who find themselves without proper spiritual direction. But it is a difficult book for the beginner: it is the product of a culture widely removed from that of the contemporary North American, and it is almost exclusively monastic in its orientation. Certain modern hesychast writings will help open the sealed treasures of the *Philokalia* to the reader.

The finest of these is the *Way of the Pilgrim*. The essence and the spirit of hesychasm are conveyed in lively, down-to-earth language (the words "hesychasm" and "hesychast" never even appear). It makes an excellent introduction to the *Philokalia*, as long as one bears in mind that it is in fact an authentic narrative of a real individual. He is simply telling his own story, and in no way suggesting that his particular method of saying the Jesus Prayer is for everybody, nor that his experiences with the Prayer are the normal experiences of all hesychasts. *The Way of the Pilgrim* must be read with sobriety and good common sense. Thus read, it is probably the most valuable book in English on the subject, apart from the *Philokalia* itself.

A modern anthology called *The Art of Prayer*, by Father Chariton of Valamo, will introduce the reader to some of the nineteenth century Russian masters of hesychasm. The English translation (also by Kadloubovsky and Palmer) has an excellent introduction by Father Kallistos (Timothy) Ware. To the English-speaking reader, Father Kallistos' introduction will be as valuable as anything else in the book, in that it sets forth in an orderly and analytical manner the basic psychological and spiritual theory underlying the hesychast approach to prayer.

There is an ever-increasing modern literature available in English now on the subject of the Jesus Prayer, much of it translations of the Russian masters of the nineteenth and twentieth centuries. In this we are most fortunate. The English-speaking reader is put in contact with the modern hesychast tradition. Many of the recent Russian hesychasts have been educated men well acquainted with the contemporary Western mentality, and able to communicate the spirit of hesychasm in terms that Western man will grasp more easily. The writings of Bishops Theophan the Recluse and Ignatius Brianchaninov in the last century, and those of Archimandrite Sophrony today, are of this type. And Archimandrite Sophrony introduces the reader to his own saintly *staretz* Silouan, a simple Russian peasant monk of Mount Athos who is one of the great *startzy* of this century.

It would be impossible here, and perhaps

superfluous, to list all the hesychast writings available in English. Most of the writers mentioned in this Appendix include bibliographies in their books. But one more book should be mentioned in this connection: *Russian Mystics* by Sergius Bolshakoff. This fine book not only puts in the hands of the English-speaking reader excerpts from Russian religious literature that would otherwise be unavailable; it also gives an excellent bibliography, guiding the interested reader to the source materials in Russian, and acquainting him with what is available in Western languages, especially English and French.